Connect Using Humor and Story

How I Got 18 Laughs 3 Applauses in a 7-Minute Persuasive Speech

Ramakrishna Reddy

DEDICATION

To Priyanka, my better half – After marrying you,
I learned more about humor than ever before

CONTENTS

INTRODUCTION

Humor, story, and persuasion are the most widely discussed elements of a speech on the public speaking circuit. There are loads and loads of information about each of these respective topics but less information on how to successfully combine these three elements into one persuasive speech. It was precisely for this reason that I wrote this book. It was the one that I had been looking for to help me when I went looking for information on how these three elements could be integrated into one speech. Like my earlier books, this book adheres to my motto: simple to understand, easy to implement. Practical information along with proven principles is distilled into a simple to understand and easy to implement approach. *One more thing*—as you read along the chapters, look for something cool. I'm offering one of my audiobooks for free so that it will act as a perfect complement for you.

Maybe you are curious to know how I was able to get eighteen laughs in a seven-minute persuasive speech and that's the reason you opened this book. But you will learn much more than that. You'll learn how to understand humor at the elemental level, how to find ways to tap into humor, how to convert real-world experiences into humorous stories, how to tie story and speech elements, along with my secret formula to craft, edit, and execute a successful persuasive speech. Not just that, we will be using a real presentation as a case study to learn these concepts. This case study helped me become one of the top three winners in a speech contest in New England. I also used a revised version of the same presentation to emerge as a top three winner at the India level. So, rest assured that this presentation has successfully undergone testing with a global audience.

If you have read my other books, you may recall my childhood story about how I went blank on stage and reacted by swearing at myself. Worse, it got amplified over the loudspeaker. It was one of the most embarrassing moments of my life and I never forgot it. Always having this memory motivated me to become a confident and articulate speaker. That's when I came across Toastmasters, the world's leading organization for improving communication and leadership skills. Initially, I had to overcome a lot, but the more I spoke on stage, the better I got. In fact, I got more excited as I learned new skills after becoming more comfortable on stage. That's when I started following the pros of public speaking such as Tony Robbins, Sir Ken Robinson, and Barack Obama. The pro speakers had this impeccable quality of being able to connect with any audience. It was during this intense learning period that I came to know about TED talks. I stumbled upon Sir Ken Robinson delivering a speech called "Schools Kill Creativity." I watched that speech like twenty times in a span of two days. This is the most watched talk on www.TED.com, and I watched it more than anybody else. Just kidding! But on a serious note, I did watch this talk, maybe a hundred times, but every time I watched it, I learned something new. However, two things stood out, which acted as evidence for its popularity and success. Those two things were story and humor. Knowing this and being able to implement them is the secret. Once I started doing this, people loved the results. It was just amazing to see the connection it created with my audience.

Initially, though I got smiles and giggles, it was hard to generate good laughs. I really wanted to learn the skill of creating humor through storytelling because it seemed like a cool skill to master. This drove me to participate in a humorous speech contest in 2010. Though it was my first time, I was determined to be good at it. I spent hours watching stand-up comedy shows, reading books, and begging people for help. Well, asking people for help. In that contest, I emerged as one of the top six speakers among the Toastmasters community in all of India and Sri Lanka. That experience made me a confident speaker.

Life moved on. I went to Connecticut in the United States to work as a consultant. After a gap of six months, I started competing. The speaking industry in the United States seemed more mature. Even though I had the raw energy, I badly needed a mentor who could control and channel it. I came to know about Jerry Aiyathurai, who happened to be the speaking champion in Connecticut, a TED speaker and a finalist of the World Championship of Public Speaking conducted by Toastmasters. I don't know if it was God's grace or sheer luck, but I connected with him in my first interaction. I have never met a kinder person. Today, I am really proud to say that he is my mentor. The thrill I got when he agreed to mentor me cannot be expressed in words. When he started mentoring me, I realized how much I did not know. He not only taught me skills but also made sure I was on track when I faced failure. In May 2012, I practiced hard for a contest and I won two levels, but lost at the third level. Jerry made sure that I got back on track. Because of that push, I again competed in the next season. Again I won two levels but lost the third level. This was a humorous speech contest, but I was pretty depressed and serious when I lost. You might be asking, "Really?" Well, humor is serious business! I thought I would never compete again. I wrote a note to the governor of the Toastmasters community in Connecticut that I was not happy with the results and how upset I was with the way the judging was done. To my surprise, instead of defending the community, she wrote me a warm email so that I did not lose heart. In fact, she went out of her way to recommend me as a speaker at a conference in upstate New York. My speech got rave reviews. It was a great feeling. In the next season, I emerged as one of the top three speakers in New England.

When I moved back to India, I continued to participate in contests. That season, I crossed five different levels and in the final level, I again emerged as one of the top three speakers in India. The next season, I participated in a contest that judged speakers on their skill in persuading an audience. Here, the message has to be strong; one could not just say funny things. The speaker has to uncover the humor from the stories and deliver it in a way that the audience would enjoy. That was a challenge that I met. In that season, I took my speech to the level of getting eighteen laughs and three rounds of applause in just seven minutes. The humor was more than situational comedy; it was carefully crafted and delivered. *I truly believe that if your speech is strong with the principles of story and humor, even a potentially boring speech will be transformed into an entertaining one.* My promise in this book is to explain how to use humor and story in a persuasive speech.

I hope you are ready for the ride. Ready, set, go.

Keep Rocking

Ramakrishna Reddy

CASE STUDY SPEECH SCRIPT: MAGIC

In which you'll see the speech script with the laugh lines and applauses marked for reference.

I stood on the edge of a long swimming pool. It was the eighteenth day my dad coached me to swim. My dad is kind and patient with everyone except me (*laugh*). He said, "Jump." I said, "I can't." He said, "Jump" (*laugh*). I said, "I can't." He goes, "Do you want to learn swimming or not?" I said, "That's what I'm thinking" (*laugh*). You see, the idea of swimming fascinated me but my hands were falling apart, my legs were falling apart, and the water was unbeatable.

Ladies and gentlemen, do you remember anything unbeatable? I remember. In my ninth grade, my classmate Vivek was unbeatable. I could never beat his rank in exams. Vivek had a big face, a thick voice, and a lot of cholesterol (*laugh*). That day— we got our results for our midterm exams. Vivek got fifth rank and I got fifteenth. Not surprising but depressing. Why? My classmates will think I am dumb (*laugh*) which I am (laugh), not (*laugh/applause*). We guys started discussing our ranks and Vivek said, "I wonder how these guys end up in top three." I said, "Vivek, even you can be in top three if you study harder." And he goes, "You know, it's not your thing. You can't even beat my rank. Just shut your mouth and leave" (*laugh*). But in front of everyone, I got humiliated. I was furious.

I went to my best buddy Rakesh and said, "I want to beat his rank. What do I do?"

He said, "Forget it" (*laugh*).

I said, "No."

He said, "Okay. I have an idea. Why don't you study every day? You will become better. You can even beat his rank."

I said, "Shall we start today?"

He said, "No. No. You study, I have to play" (*laugh*).

Do you have such friends? … God bless you (*laugh*).

That evening—my friends called me to play cricket, I said "No."

My sister called me to watch TV, I said "No."

My mom called me to eat Maggi, I said, "Yes" (*laugh*).

After eating, I picked up my book to study. I studied and studied and studied till I fell asleep after five minutes (*laugh*). I started to sleep but could not continue to sleep. The humiliation became my nightmare. I woke up and cried, again and again. I studied so that I could stop crying. And I studied every single day. After a few months, exams came. Then the results came and guess what? Vivek got the sixth rank and I got the second rank in my class. My teacher was shocked. Vivek was shocked. I was shocked (*laugh*). It was like magic (*applause*).

Fast-forward fourteen years; if you were sitting with me in that coffee shop, you would have seen my best buddy Rakesh and me, sipping freshly brewed cappuccino and recalling that school incident.

Rakesh said, "Rama, do you know how you created that magic at school?"

I said, "Hard work."

He goes, "No, it's because of your habit of studying every single day. Habits create magic."

That's when it hit me—I was missing the magic of good habits in my life. I needed it badly to beat those things that seemed unbeatable. You know what was the first thing that came to my mind? Swimming. Why? Since childhood, swimming fascinated me but the water daunted me. My dad being a swimmer, I asked, "Dad, will you coach me to swim?" He said, "No, lazy bone." To make him say "Yes," I promised him that I would practice swimming for one hour every single day. Sounds simple; but was really painful. I was bruised and battered for seventeen continuous days. And on the eighteenth day, I stood on the edge of a long swimming pool. My hands were falling apart, my legs were falling apart, and the water was unbeatable. But my habits gave me that push to plunge into the pool. I gasped for breath, fluttered my hands and legs as fast as possible, and I started to sink (*laugh*). Even under water, I tried again and again and again. And all of a sudden, I started floating. I beat the water, sprang to the surface, and started beating on and on and on till I reached the far end of the long swimming pool. It was like magic.

What seems unbeatable in your life?

Maybe staying in shape seems unbeatable—a habit of working out 30 minutes every day can create the magic.

Maybe growing as a speaker seems unbeatable—a habit of competing in every speech contest can create the magic.

Maybe being an ideal husband seems unbeatable—a habit of saying "I love you" (*laugh*) 50 times (*laugh*) every day (*laugh*) cannot create the magic (*applause*). Listening to her 50 times can create the magic (*applause*).

Friends, in the swimming pool of your life, you might fall apart; you might struggle; you might even sink in the water that seems unbeatable. But you can beat the unbeatable using habits because "habits create magic."

CHAPTER 1

STORY, HUMOR, AND PERSUASION SIMPLIFIED

In which I explain Aristotle's view on persuasion, perspectives about humor, and persuasive storytelling with humor

What makes a great story? A great story is when an ordinary character overcomes seemingly impossible circumstances to achieve a goal. That's it. If you can understand this sentence and digest each and every word and reflect it in your story creation process, you are already halfway into creating exciting content.

Now, what is humor? In simple terms, humor brings amusement and laughter to a speech so that the audience is entertained.

Then what is persuasion? In the context of a speech, persuasion is the speaker's skill at influencing how the audience thinks, feels, or acts as a result of hearing the speech.

Persuasion from Aristotle

Aristotle in his masterpiece *Rhetoric* wrote that persuasion is the result of ethos, logos, and pathos. To be concise, ethos is credibility, pathos is the emotional connect, and logos is the logic in your speech. The best way to use these three elements when speaking is through a *personal* story. Why a personal story, and not just any story? When you speak, you need credibility (ethos) and that's what comes through in a personal story. If it is the story of your own life, you have the right to speak about it with authority. Logic (logos) can be taken care of by carefully crafting your speech content with the proper flow of ideas in a good order. The emotional connect (pathos) is the main reason for using a story. Story is a powerhouse for pathos because stories have the unique ability to transmit emotion. Emotion creates a great connection with the audience. And on top of it, if you add humor, you will hit a home run.

I can tell that humor and story are the greatest tools for any speaker. Story has the power to transmit emotion and humor helps to deliver positive emotions. Hence, humorous stories make for one of the best mediums to connect with an audience. A great story has a life of its own. With a great story, your words walk into the hearts of your listeners. When you add humor, your words will fly into the hearts of your listeners.

Perspectives of Humor

Dr. Charles Jarvis, a dentist, humorist, and Hall of Fame speaker, defined humor as "the mental faculty of discovering, expressing or appreciating the ludicrous or absurdly incongruous." Jarvis shared two additional definitions of humor with us. The first is "a painful thing told playfully." The second is "tragedy separated by time and space." Note that both definitions treat humor as a serious thought viewed in a light manner. Ever heard someone say, "I laughed so hard I nearly cried"? This shows how close humor is to pathos: an emotion of sympathetic pity.

The other theory, which is really cool, is the benign violation theory coined by Dr. Peter McGraw and Joel Warner. I heard this theory from McGraw's TED talk "What Makes Things Funny." Although he is not a stand-up comedian, he has done a lot of research on humor. According to the duo, humor gets created when there is a benign (harmless or safe) violation from what is acceptable. They illustrate this theory by using the old gag of someone slipping on a banana peel. Such an accident usually elicits a laugh. However, if the person was hurt badly in the fall, it won't elicit a laugh because it has become harmful and the playful element has been lost.

Sophie Scott in her TED talk "Why We Laugh" said, "When you are alone, you do not laugh often. It means the humor creation is beyond just the quality of the joke. You laugh because you say that you understand the speaker and you agree with the speaker." Humor creates a strong bond and is a vital element for connection. When an audience laughs, it means more than just being entertained; their laughter says they understand you, they like you.

Persuasive Story with Humor

Now that we understand perspectives of humor, let's understand perspectives about story. There are many types of stories and as I mentioned earlier, it would be a cool idea to focus on using a personal story for persuasion. You can persuade even without humor if you tell a moving story of someone dying in your arms, or how you climbed Mt. Everest, or fought with a tiger, etc., but if you, like me, don't have such an emotional story, humor is your *mantra*.

In order to inject humor into your speech in an organic way, you need to learn the skills needed to craft a persuasive story. Did you notice that I used the word *skills?* That is because knowing how to craft a persuasive story requires skills. That's the reason I am about to carefully lead you through a tested persuasive and humorous speech. Along the way, we will uncover its secrets and strategies and you will learn the nuts and bolts of how it was created so that you can create your own humorous and persuasive stories. You will also learn the secrets to editing and delivering your speech in ways which will keep your audience engaged and entertained.

CHAPTER 2

KNOWING THE EQUATION FOR CREATING LAUGH LINES

*In which I explain **premise, pause, punch line, pause** and how they work together to create a laugh line*

Some people are so talented that humor just pours out of them. And then there are those like me! Many people think creating humor is hard, but actually it is not. Being humorous on stage is a skill you can master if you are willing to work at it. To begin, here is something that you can use. There are many variations to the following humor equation and they can all work because people laugh at different things for different reasons. The following, however, is a good one to follow for crafting laugh lines within a speech.

Premise + Pause + Punch Line + Pause = Laughter

Let us understand the elements with a laugh line.

People exaggerate that parents in India pressure their children to only become a doctor or an engineer. That's not true. They don't just pressure. They blackmail.

I have rewritten the above laugh line to indicate the different elements of humor.

> *People exaggerate that parents in India pressure their children to only become a doctor or an engineer. That's not true. They don't just pressure.* <Pause 1> They blackmail <Pause 2>.

Premise: The premise is the information needed for an audience to understand or appreciate the punch line. In our example, words highlighted in italics form the premise. The premise must:

- Be believable, even if not completely true. In our example, the premise is believable because the audience also could agree it is a cultural thing that Indian parents are pretty hard on their child's ambition.

- Lead the audience in one direction (in order to surprise them later). Note that I said, "That's not true. They don't just pressure." This leads the audience to think that I am going to say something positive about Indian parents.

- Not be funny.

- Be easily understood.

- Create anticipation in the minds of the audience.

- Be relevant for the audience.

- Be about a situation with which the audience can identify and empathize.

Pause 1: Is needed to build tension. Pause 1 must:

- Heighten the curiosity.

- Not be so long that the audience members lose interest.

- Be long enough to create tension. This is what is known as *timing*.

Punch Line: It is a word or phrase that follows the pause that triggers laughter. Punch line should create surprise by *saying something contrary to the audience's expectation.* Here, the punch line is, "They blackmail." The laughter is the result of the release of the tension built up during the pause.

Pause 2: This pause gives the audience time to laugh. Again, it's the timing that is important in comedy and many speakers make the mistake of not pausing after they trigger the laugh. If you do not pause, you will be cutting the laughter short. Don't do this—enjoy it and let the audience enjoy it, too.

Also, during this pause for laughter, you can get the most out of it by using gestures or even a deadpan expression to maximize the effect. Try different gestures to see which one works best.

CHAPTER 3

REAL-WORLD EXPERIENCE INTO A HUMOROUS STORY

In which I explain how to relate real-life experiences so they come across as funny

The method we'll cover for converting any real experience, observation, or scenario into a humorous story or anecdote has worked very well for me and those whom I have coached. There is no reason it shouldn't work for you as well.

It helps to at least understand the process of stand-up comedy and an easy way to do this is to read *The Comedy Bible* by Judy Carter. This book certainly helped me. Even though I had no intention of becoming a stand-up comic, the rules helped me. When I applied Carter's stand-up strategy to my storytelling, I struck the humor gold mine. Right, now we both are aligned to the point: Humor is gold!

In the previous chapter we learned the equation for humor—premise, pause, punch line, pause. The following process will show you how to create punch lines to deliver laughs from personal *experiences*. This process can be used not only for sharing your *experiences* but also used for sharing your *perspectives* about your life. Here's the high-level process.

Step 1: Write down the raw story or your thoughts.

Step 2: From the raw piece of content,

a) Find topic and create topic introduction.

b) Find attitude and create attitude statement.

c) Find point of view and create point of view statement.

d) Find humor trigger and create relevant experience.

Don't worry if you don't understand any of the terms mentioned above. I'll come back to it soon.

Step 3: Sequence the topic introduction, attitude statement, point of view statement, and relevant experience.

Let me walk you through the whole process with an example so that it is easier to understand.

First Example

Step 1: Write

First, write down the story as you remember it—this is the raw story. Here's my example:

> A few months ago, after finishing my assignment, I was traveling back from New York, USA, to Chennai, India. I went to the ticketing counter and gave my passport to get my boarding pass. The officer looked at my passport and said, "Ramakrishna Reddy Veerappa Narayana

Reddy. Sir, it seems you have used all alphabets in English language." I smiled but felt embarrassed because of his comment on my name.

Step 2: Find and Create

a) Find topic and create the topic introduction

Find topic: You can find the topic from the raw story by focusing on the main theme of the story. While zeroing in on the topic, you need to determine whether the topic is leading to the rest of the story. Also, the topic should be relatable to your audience. The above points are applicable even if the raw content is not about an experience but about your perspective about something that seems funny. In this particular story, topic is my "long name."

Create the topic Introduction: For our example, we had identified the topic as "long name." Let us talk about creating a topic introduction. For the humor to work, first you need to warm up the audience with the topic. For that, you need to clearly introduce the topic so that they have necessary information to appreciate the humor. Hence, for our example, the audience needs to be aware that I already have a long name. After some thought, I felt I could use my passport as a transition tool to tell the audience that my name is pretty long in it. Here's how I created the topic introduction.

> Ramakrishna Reddy is not my complete name. My name in passport says, "Ramakrishna Reddy Veerappa Narayana Reddy."

b) Find attitude and create attitude statement

Find attitude: In *The Comedy Bible,* Judy Carter says that trying to create comedy without attitude is like driving a car without gas. This explains why certain punch lines result in huge laughs and others do not. This is an example of how a concept so simple isn't always evident until it is pointed out. I find it awesome when this happens. I followed Carter's suggestion of attitude words: *hard, weird, stupid,* and *scary.* By using any of these words, you are deliberately giving attitude to your story. Pros don't use attitude words, but they show attitude with body language, facial expressions, and gestures. I recommend you use the textbook approach. Begin by using these attitude words and work up to conveying attitude through non-verbal methods as you become more experienced.

Create attitude statement: *Creating an attitude statement is to convey how you feel about your topic.* It means selecting the right attitude word and applying it in a way to elicit a humorous response. Since my goal is to convert a real story to a humorous one, I use the type of situation to help me find the best word to create the attitude. To do this, let's use the four attitude words suggested by Carter to ask the following questions about the topic:

What is *hard* about a long name?

What is *weird* about a long name?

What is *stupid* about a long name?

What is *scary* about a long name?

Considering my situation at the airport, the words *hard* and *weird* seem to work best. Now we need to narrow it down to one word and *hard* is the word that rings the truest. As we saw earlier, attitude statement needs to convey how you feel about your topic. Topic is "long name." Attitude is "hard." Combine both of them and you have the attitude statement as "Long names are hard."

c) Find point of view and create a point of view statement

Find point of view: Point of view is your analysis of what happened. You'll be able to come up with point of view by thinking about the reason why you are complaining. It should answer why *you* are conveying the attitude you have chosen. My point of view was that the "Officer was making fun of me."

Create a point of view statement: I have realized that this statement can play two roles. In the first role, which is in this case, it can help you set a clear premise before you say the relevant experience. The relevant experience part will have the *punch line*. In the second role, which is the second example following this, point of view statement will have the *punch line* because the humor trigger is part of point of view.

For this example, point of view statement is setting a clear premise. Hence, make sure the statement is generic. The key is—understand this carefully—your story has to become your audience's story. You can do this when you *generalize the situation and put the audience in the setup. There is a simple way to achieve this.* Just replace the pronouns "I" or "me" with "you."

Hence the point of view "Officer was making fun of me" becomes "People make fun of you" or "People mock you." You need to use words that an audience relates to in daily life. In this instance, the better choice is "People make fun of you."

d) Find humor trigger and create relevant experience

Find humor trigger: Trigger is what creates the funniness. It is what cracks you up. You can find the trigger by highlighting the exact word or phrase that you think is having the funny quotient. In the above example, "Sir, it seems you have used all alphabets in English language" is what I felt was funny.

Create relevant experience: There is a reason why we extracted the humor trigger. This is because we need to include only relevant things about our experience, which will naturally lead to the humor trigger. Creating relevant experience is a critical process to tighten up your speech. Let us see how this applies to our story.

Let me write down points that can be excluded from the raw story:

- Why I am traveling.

- Action of going to the counter and giving boarding pass.

Let me write down points that can be included from the raw story:

- We need to tell that the place is an airport.

- We also need to tell that the airport is in New York. Only then can the audience assume that it is an American officer who could not pronounce my name properly.

Based on the above ideas, I created relevant experience as shown below:

> For instance, an officer at New York airport looked at my passport and goes, "Ramakrishna Reddy Veerappa Narayana Reddy. Sir, it seems you have used all alphabets in English language."

Step 3: Sequence

As discussed earlier, we will be sequencing topic introduction, attitude statement, point of view statement, and relevant experience to form the humorous anecdote. Excited to see the formation of a humorous anecdote? Here we go!

> Ramakrishna Reddy is not my complete name. My name in passport says, "Ramakrishna Reddy Veerappa Narayana Reddy." Long names are hard. People make fun of you. For instance, an officer at New York airport looked at my passport and goes, "Ramakrishna Reddy Veerappa Narayana Reddy. Sir, it seems you have used all alphabets in English language."

The above formula might not always hand over a perfect humorous story. You need to be ready to tweak your sentences to tighten the flow of the story. For example, in the above story, adding the question "Why?" between "Long names are hard" and "People make fun of you" tightens the flow. Again, the effectiveness also depends on delivery, which is what we are going to see next.

Delivery

Constructing a humorous story is one thing, delivering it effectively is another. Construction and delivery have to be in sync. We constructed the humorous story by putting together the topic introduction, attitude statement, point of view statement, and relevant experience. Now, to deliver it effectively, view the whole entity from the premise, pause, punch line, pause perspective. To do this, start by identifying all the words that contribute to the premise and to the punch line.

The premise:

> Ramakrishna Reddy is not my complete name. My name in passport says, "Ramakrishna Reddy Veerappa Narayana Reddy." Long names are hard. Why? People make fun of you. For instance, an officer at New York airport looked at my passport and goes "Ramakrishna Reddy Veerappa Narayana Reddy…"

The long length of this premise is okay since the objective is to learn to use humor in stories, not to become a stand-up comic. When delivering the premise, the objective is to be sincere and honest, not funny. Say it as you would talk to a friend. Use optimum movement and gestures to convey your premise clearly. I started moving and gesturing only when I started speaking about the officer. I mimed as the officer looking at the passport, I faked an American accent and said "Ramakrishna Reddy Veerappa Narayana Reddy," and gave a few weird looks and then… <paused>

Pausing After Premise:

As we discussed earlier, pausing after the premise creates curiousness, anticipation and tension. Even if the quality of the premise and the punch line is top-notch, your audience won't laugh without this pause. In this case, I paused for two to three seconds.

The Punch Line:

"Sir, it seems you have used all alphabets in the English language."

Since you are expecting the audience to laugh at the end of the punch line, you need to be creative during your delivery. While delivering the punch line, I used an American accent and wore a silly smile. This is where you pull out all the stops and use intonation, exaggeration, modulation, body movement, and facial expressions to your advantage. Try different things and choose the one that elicits the best results. Practice makes perfect. Being funny is all about testing and tweaking your material.

Pausing After Punch Line:

A good rule of thumb is to pause for a second or two and see if you get any response. If you do get a response, *continue to pause* and let them laugh till the entire audience finishes laughing. If not, move on at the same pace as you would if you were just continuing with the speech. This time will vary. One second, two seconds or three seconds? Well, it depends. You'll pick up the skill of pausing as you deliver more laugh lines during actual presentations. You'll also get good at it if you deliberately pause when practicing for your presentation.

A Second Example

Let's follow our three-step process to construct a humorous anecdote. As I said earlier, this is a case where the point of view is strong enough to serve as your punch line. Let's see how it goes.

Step 1 – Write the raw story or perspective as it is. Here you go:

A few years after starting my career as a software engineer, my dad was asking me to get married. In India, parents find the bride or groom and marriages are arranged. (Hold on, that is not the joke.) I was very anxious about an arranged marriage because you never know how your life will turn out. And then, one day during work hours I was testing a piece of code when the thought "How nice it would be if we had an option to do testing before getting married" struck me. *I felt that thought was funny.*

Step 2 – From the raw story or perspective, **find and create.**

a) Find topic and create topic introduction

Find topic: We need to find topic in such a way that it is relatable and leads to the trigger. From that reasoning perspective, *marriage* seems to be our topic.

Creating topic introduction: Marriage is such a common thing that you can get creative in introducing the topic. One idea is to use relevant experience for creating the topic introduction. For instance, for our example, I picked a specific instance where my dad is asking me to get married. Let's see how I introduced the topic:

Few weeks ago, my dad said, "Rama, get married." I said, "No."

b) Find attitude and create attitude statement

Find attitude: Remember, comedy queen Judy Carter advised on four attitude words: *hard, weird, scary,* and *stupid.* To find which attitude applies to a situation, do a quick check of how the character is feeling towards the topic. Is the character feeling that something is hard, weird, scary, or stupid? As the writer, you have to take that call. I felt *scary* seemed to be the best choice. Read the raw perspective from Step 1 again. Imagine the character's situation. It makes more sense when the attitude word is *scary.*

Create attitude statement: Creating the attitude statement is easy. Just use the attitude word to describe your topic. Attitude is *scary* and topic is *marriage.* So, we have attitude statement as "Marriages are scary." Since I am planning to deliver point of view specific to my case (not generic as seen in earlier example), I changed the attitude statement to suit the same. Again, this depends on your preference and what makes more sense. Another thing that I want to mention is that if you feel that the audience needs to get more information to appreciate the *punch line*, be more specific and emphasize the attitude again. I felt that I could take my audience deeper. Hence I added, "I have fears." So the attitude statement is:

I have fears. I am scared of marriage.

c) Find point of view and create point of view statement

Find point of view: As seen earlier, *point of view is your analysis of the situation.* To find the exact words, you need to answer why you are saying the attitude statement. Let's try to answer using our example. I said that attitude statement "I have fears. I am scared of marriage" because even though I am a software engineer I would be marrying someone without doing testing of our life with each other. Hence the point of view is "Though I am a software engineer, I would be marrying someone without doing testing."

Creating point of view statement: Point of view is "Though I am a software engineer, I would be marrying someone without doing testing." This is going to help us create point of view statement, which will include the punch line.

In the earlier example, the punch line was present in the relevant experience part. The dialogue "Sir, it seems you have used all alphabets in English language" by the airport officer created humor. Our dialogue as it is functioned as our punch line. In this case (where humor trigger is part of point of view), we should create punch line by slightly modifying the point of view. A simple rule for creating punch line is to keep minimum words that encapsulate the humor trigger. Our point of view is "Though I am a software engineer, I would be marrying someone without doing testing." The core idea that is triggering humor is "getting married without testing." This line can be modified from first person's perspective to: "I can't go live without testing." "I am a software guy" is necessary but can be split as a separate sentence.

So, our entire point of view statement is "I am a software engineer. I can't go live without testing."

Step 3 – Sequence

In the first example, we sequenced topic introduction, attitude statement, point of view statement, and relevant experience. In this case, we created our punch line in point of view statement itself.

Topic introduction – Few weeks ago, my dad said, "Rama, get married." I said, "No."

Attitude statement – I have fears. I am scared of marriage.

Point of view statement – I am a software guy. I can't go live without testing.

After sequencing, here we go with the humorous anecdote:

> Few weeks ago, my dad said "Rama, get married." I said, "No." I have fears. I am scared of marriage. I am a software guy. I can't go live without testing.

I can use the above piece in any speech where the topic is about marriage. This always works for me.

You see, even though punch lines on the surface seem to be simple and straightforward, they aren't. It will take some time to get tuned to this concept, but be patient. Apply yourself when you write and practice your anecdotes. Practice your timing so that you pause for maximum effect. Everything won't be perfect at the first go, but I can tell you for sure that you'll get better, as you practice and tweak your punch lines to get a laugh.

Delivery

We constructed the humorous anecdote by putting together the topic introduction, attitude statement, and point of view statement. Now, to deliver the same, it is time to view the whole entity from the premise, pause, punch line, pause perspective. Start identifying all the words that contribute to the premise and to the punch line. Before reading further, try finding premise and punch line.

The premise is:

> Few weeks ago, my dad said, "Get married." I said, "No." I have fears. I am scared of marriage. I am a software guy.

When delivering the premise, the objective is to be sincere and honest, not funny. I used optimum movement and gestures to convey the premise and then <paused>.

Pausing after premise:

As we discussed earlier, pausing after the premise creates curiousness, anticipation, and tension. Even if the quality of the premise and punch line is top-notch, your audience won't laugh without this pause. In this case, I paused for two to three seconds. The punch line is:

> I can't go live without testing.

While delivering the punch line, I had an attitude of intense anxiousness. Since you are expecting the audience to laugh at the end of the punch line, you need to be creative during your delivery. This is where you pull out all the stops and use intonation, exaggeration, modulation, body movement, and facial expressions to your advantage. Try different things and choose the one that elicits the best results. Practice makes perfect. Being funny is all about testing and tweaking your material.

Pausing after punch line:

I usually have a deadpan expression during this pause. This punch line gets me maximum laughs. Hence I pause till the audience is completely done with laughter.

CHAPTER 4

SYNERGIZING SPEECH AND STORY STRUCTURE

In which you'll learn about selecting stories, suspended story technique, and a formula for speech-story structure integration

As you probably know by now, I am biased towards using personal stories in speeches. When you are starting out, this gives you a huge advantage and jump-start in composing your speech. However, should all stories in your speech be core personal stories? Not really. You can use third party stories. But try to use those with a personal link between you and the event you are talking about.

For example, maybe you are using a friend's story, or even retelling one from a famous personality. It makes the most sense to use only stories of people with whom you have interacted on some level. If you do choose to use a story where you have no connection at all, at least make sure the story can support your message. At the end of the day, all the stories in your speech need to support your overall message.

Why do you need multiple stories for a speech and not a single story? Well, different stories add variety and weight to your message. They add depth, dimension, and impact to your presentation. Of course, if you are giving only a short speech, it may be better to focus on a single story. If you have more stories in reserve, you can tailor the length of your speech to the time you have.

How to Select Stories

The following is how I went about selecting a story for one of my speeches. The first thing we all need to do is come up with an idea or message. One way to settle on a *message* is to introspect whether you are exhibiting any trait. Get deep into traits that you exhibit and judge what would be useful to the audience. In my case, one trait that kept coming back was "Laugh at yourself during embarrassing situation."

To prove that message, the story I settled on was one about taking my friend who is a girl (not girlfriend) on a motorcycle ride and running out of gas—very embarrassing and tricky to manage! In the middle of the road she looked at me and asked, "What is your plan of action?" Usually it's my manager who asks me this question. Even though the situation was not funny at the time, I later found it hilarious when I thought about it. This event triggered the message I wanted to give which was "Laugh at yourself when you are in embarrassing situations." Whenever I get caught in embarrassing situations, even though the actual event might be stressful at that moment, I try to laugh at my embarrassing position. Over a period of time, I managed to live my life with the ability to laugh at myself and it worked well both for me and for anyone in that situation with me. It was something that resonated with me.

So, I created a speech with that message, "Laugh at yourself."

Once I zeroed in on this theme, I started jotting down my embarrassing moments at school, at home, and at college. Even though I had many stories, I selected one from my college days because college is a memorable time in most people's lives.

A few days later, when someone referenced the story of *Mahabharata* (the longest known epic), another idea struck. There is an important incident in the epic where the chief antagonist Dhuryodhana develops animosity towards the Pandava queen Dhrowpathi because she laughed at him when he fell into a pond because the pond was disguised as colored art. The story was a good example of how the message "Laugh at yourself" could have changed the course of things in the epic. You don't always *have* to choose from personal stories, but can also choose any story that supports your message.

If you need ideas to find speech topics for persuasive speeches, you are going to love what is going to come. Please visit www.publicspeakKing.com/connecttopic and download the *Public Speaking Topic Secrets* audiobook for free. It is an audiobook which people are currently paying to buy. I just wanted to offer you this for free because you have made an investment to read this book. I like to keep it that way.

Stories for the Case Study Speech

This case study is comprised of two stories. The first one is from my childhood.

My classmate insulted me for scoring low marks. I studied hard every day and beat his rank in the next exam. Only later, I real-

ized that good habits were the secret to that success.

The reason I selected this story was it had a lot of impact in my life. In fact, this story changed the way I started doing things. And moreover, the background of the story seemed relatable to the audience.

The second story is about how I learned to swim.

I wanted to learn to swim so I went to the pool every day with my dad. I was scared. My dad was a tough coach. The water was scary. I felt like giving up. However, my dad pushed me to continue every day. After a few weeks, I started to swim. I learned that persistence gives you results.

The reason I chose this story was because it seemed to be a good fit to apply the message I learned in the earlier story.

Would the speech be interesting if I recounted the stories as I did above? Certainly not, so it's time to learn how to craft a persuasive and humorous speech using these stories.

Speech Structure and Essential Elements

As we all know, the most important function of structure is to add shape and support something—in this case, your presentation. The first step in creating content is determining a suitable structure in which you'll organize and present your content.

The following is the basic skeletal structure of a speech.

Opening... *transition*

Context setting... *transition*

[Key point or core message

Supporting point

Application of the key point or core message]... *transition*

Summary... *transition*

Conclusion

Note that key point or core message, supporting point, and application are listed here for reference purposes. However, for all practical purposes, they are pretty fluid in nature. You'll learn this soon when I synergize the story and speech structure.

Let us learn more about the elements of a speech.

Opening is what you say in the first 30 or 60 seconds.

Context setting is explaining what you are going to tell them. Sometimes, this part gets merged into your opening.

Key point helps to reinforce the core message of your talk. Sometimes you'll have three or four key points in a talk. In that case, all the key points should point to the same core message. For our case study speech, there is only one key point. Hence key point and core message are the same.

Supporting point is to substantiate or prove the key point. You can use stories, statistics, illustration, or facts for support. You can use any or all of these for support. For our case study, I have used *only* two stories.

Application specifically tells the audience how to apply the key point or core message in their life.

Summary drives home what you have told them and recaps your presentation. Sometimes, it gets combined with conclusion.

Conclusion is the showstopper for your presentation. This is the final 30 or 60 seconds of your presentation.

Transitions maintain a smooth and clear flow between the opening, context setting, key points, supporting points, summary, and conclusion. If a speech is like a multi-storied building, then transitions are like the escalators to seamlessly take you to different floors.

Now, that we learned about the elements and a basic speech structure, let us customize it. In our case study speech, I used only two stories—that's it. No facts, statistics, or illustrations. The key point and core message are the same—"Habits create magic."

Now, I want to take a few minutes to talk about the overall story structure. I am not talking about how to arrange the elements of the story; we'll do that in a bit, but for now remember that to persuade, your speech should be built on a solid structure of your stories. After studying a lot of speeches, I realized why some speeches had me hooked and why some did not. The speeches that got me hooked were always constructed around a solid story structure.

When I was researching structure while writing my speech, I read an article by Mark Brown, 1995 World Champion of Public Speaking. He talked about the suspended story structure. I immediately got hooked and applied this for our case study speech. It goes like this:

> Start Story 1... Suspend Story 1.
>
> Start Story 2... Complete Story 2.
>
> Continue Story 1... Complete Story 1.

Essential Elements of a Persuasive Story

If a speech has its regular elements, a persuasive story also has its essential elements. The following are the essential elements of a persuasive story.

1) Character

2) Conflict

3) Obstacles

4) Change

5) Resolution

If you just make sure that these elements are present in your story, you *have* a good story with a strong structure in place. Story is such a beautiful and useful thing. It can act as a canvas to incorporate the elements of a regular speech. For this case study, I took this suspended story technique, used all essential elements of a story (character, conflict, obstacles, change, and resolution), and developed a formula that fits the regular elements of a speech structure. This is exciting because we are going to combine both and show how a persuasive speech is developed! Let's get started.

Synergizing Speech and Story Structure

The formula used here is to synergize the stories and the speech structure. This formula was created using the concept of the suspended story structure. The elements of "Speech" are in *italics*. This way it is easier to differentiate speech elements and understand how the elements of the speech and story are getting integrated. This formula has worked for me. Feel free to experiment by taking this as a base. So, here we go:

The speech *opening* was an amusing scene from swimming story where we introduce characters (protagonist, antagonist, and supporting characters), show the conflict, and set the *context*…

… *Transition*… to childhood story

Introduce new characters, show the conflict, heighten obstacles, and show the change after overcoming obstacles…

… *Transition*… to swimming story

Bring out the *key point or message* as the resolution (this is more like the secret of how you overcame obstacles) of childhood story. Show benefit of message. *Apply* the key point or message in swimming story. Heighten the obstacles; show the change after overcoming obstacles…

… *Transition*… to *summary* by relating the obstacles in your story to the obstacles in your audience's life, then *conclude* your speech by telling your audience to adopt your *key point or message* as the solution to overcome their obstacles.

In the next chapter, we'll expand this formula and show every device and technique used to create eighteen laughs and three rounds of applause in the seven-minute persuasive speech.

CHAPTER 5

THE POWERFUL SPEECH OPENING

In which I'll show how to create a powerful opening using story along with character introductions, conflicts, and humor

Speech Opening

There are various techniques you can use to open a speech. Story is the most powerful technique but asking a question, giving a statistic, or making a statement (or using a quote) are also effective. For now, we will focus on the story as the opening to the presentation. Having said that, it is not helpful just to say that you start off with a story. How should you really start a story? The first few lines are the most important and should follow the key rule: *Your audience needs to be oriented to your story.* You should set the scene before the scene. It is more like giving details about where, when, who or what that every story needs in order to make some sense. For example, whether you are talking about a person sitting at home on a Saturday morning or a person at work on a Friday evening. I understand that you might argue that we should not give away the audience's curiosity. But the point is that you have to give the bare minimum information for the audience to form images and try to visualize the scene that you are presenting. If you miss this initial connection with your audience, the rest of the speech won't be effective. Let us look at the opening of the case study speech that helps the audience visualize the setting for the story they are about to hear.

> I stood on the edge of the long swimming pool. It was the eighteenth day my dad coached me to swim.

I could have given more information (I would recommend doing so if time is not a constraint), but the above lines served the purpose as it was a competitive speech and economy of words played a critical role.

Introducing the Characters

The three most important characters in any story are the protagonist, the supporting character, and the antagonist. The protagonist is the main character around which the story is built. It is a good rule of thumb to have your protagonist as yourself or a person close to you. Supporting character is someone who helps the protagonist in the journey to overcome obstacles and achieve his or her goal. A supporting character can be a person, pet, or even an inanimate object like a book. In my swimming story, my dad is the supporting character. Also note that the protagonist and supporting character (me and my dad) were introduced right away in the first few sentences. Antagonist introduction is also important because it introduces someone who can potentially prevent the protagonist from achieving his or her goal. An antagonist need not necessarily be limited to a person. For persuasive speeches, it could be a bad habit, big ego, or fear. In the swimming story, it was my fear of water.

Now, that we have an idea of characters, let's remember our goal, which is to make the audience cheer for the protagonist. I am going to share a secret for this. *Put the protagonist in situations to which the audience can relate.* A person struggling to learn swimming is one such situation. That's exactly how we started the speech and also introduced all three characters.

Showcase the Conflict

> My dad is kind and patient with everyone except me. He said, "Jump." I said, "I can't." He said, "Jump." I said, "I can't." He goes, "Do you want to learn swimming or not?" I said, "That's what I'm thinking." You see, the idea of swimming fascinated me but my hands were falling apart, my legs were falling apart, and the water was unbeatable.

This is how my story continued. Observe how I am immediately showing the conflict. It's because the power of the conflict hooks the audience. Here I am, trembling on the edge of a swimming pool with my dad pressuring me to jump in the pool. The stage is set. I am introducing two levels of conflict. One is between my dad and me. The other is between the water and me. The takeaway is that you need to *show the conflict of your story as soon as possible.*

Creating Laughs During Conflict

Conflict doesn't always need to be serious; humor works just as well and often better. In fact, your greatest laugh line can come from moments of conflict. I want to destroy the myth that conflict needs to have a serious background. Even in a serious speech, there is always an opportunity to create some organic humor.

Let's see how the humor was created during this conflict. During the actual experience, my dad asked me to jump a couple of times but I did not reply. Instead, I kept thinking, why did I decide to learn swimming from him? This idea seemed funny to me. But I needed to find a way to convert this raw idea into humor. I did this by making notes on what happened in real time and tightening them up. However, it is very important to *first identify the trigger for humor*. In this case, my dad telling me "Jump" again and again while I am regretting asking him to coach me is the trigger. However, if I just say it in the way that I wrote it right now, it will only fetch me giggles or smiles. In order to get laughs, we need to channel the idea through the humor tools. Let me introduce you to my favorite tool—Rule of Three.

Rule of Three

Rule of Three is a communication device that falls under the umbrella of rhetorical devices. I want to take a moment and tell you about rhetorical devices. These are among the best-kept secrets for implementing persuasion in speeches or written content. The Wikipedia definition says, "*A rhetorical device is a technique that an author or speaker uses to convey to the listener or reader a meaning with the goal of persuading him or her towards considering a topic from a different perspective, using sentences designed to encourage or provoke a rational argument from an emotional display of a given perspective or action. Note that although rhetorical devices may be used to evoke an emotional response in the audience, this is not their primary purpose."*

I'll soon cover a number of rhetorical devices as we come to their specific usage. But now, let's focus on Rule of Three, which is used to present an idea or data in three parts to make it easy for the listener to follow and remember. In my speeches, I use it left, right, and center. (You just saw the Rule of Three in action!)

Why three? Well, two seems *less* to make an impact and four seems *more* to remember. Nothing scientific here or complicated, I used this more than any other device and it always works like a charm.

In order to leverage this concept in your humor creation process, do this:

Let us say that we have three items—Item 1, Item 2, and Item 3. In order to create humor, the first two items should be something that the audience is expecting and the last item should be something that the audience is not expecting. In other words, Rule of Three for humor creation can be interpreted as *expected, expected*, and *unexpected*. You can use expected, expected to lead them in one direction and use the unexpected to create the punch.

Now, see Rule of Three for humor in action in our case study sample.

First part: He said, "Jump." I said, "I can't." (expected)

Second part: He said, "Jump." I said, "I can't.'" (expected)

Third part: He goes, "Do you want to learn swimming or not?"

I said, "That's what I'm thinking." (unexpected—this where the unexpected comes into play. This is the part where you twist and create the laughs.)

One more example: This principle is so powerful that it also works when you break a straight sentence and deliver it in threes. Take a look at the following example.

First part: My dad is kind and patient (expected)

Second part: with everyone (expected)

Third part: except me (unexpected)

Just use this device and see the results for yourself. Even if you do not get a laugh, at least your ideas will be understandable and memorable.

Next, let us understand another application of Rule of Three. I used this one to set the clear conflict between the swimming pool water and me. Here, we are not using this tool to create humor. We are using this tool to clearly convey the idea that I was tired and lacking confidence to jump in the pool.

First part: My hands were falling apart

Second part: my legs were falling apart

Third part: and the water was unbeatable

Once you know the power of Rule of Three, you will love using it in your speeches.

CHAPTER 6

CONTEXT SETTING, TRANSITIONS, AND HUMOR DEVICES

In which you'll learn metaphorical transformation technique for context setting, transition using word play and metaphor, and creating humor using character descriptions

Context Setting

Context setting is about planning what you are about to say—setting the stage, so to speak. This is an important step which many people overlook when forming a speech. The common reason for this is the feeling of giving the speech away too early and the audience losing interest. However, nothing is further from the truth. As the speaker, it is your responsibility to give an idea about the subject of your talk. That's your promise to your audience. Doing this really helps to build the *connection.* I am going to share a secret for achieving the same. *Convert the problem in your story into a problem in your audience's story.* By doing this, you persuade them to think about a problem in their life as I did in the case study speech:

Ladies and gentlemen, do you remember anything unbeatable in your life?

Observe the things that are in play here and see that I used a device called metaphorical transformation. This is really cool because in one or two sentences you can convert the problem in your story into a problem that your audience can relate to in their own life. You need a metaphor and a question to implement this.

Metaphorical Transfer

A metaphor is a figure of speech that identifies something as being the same as some unrelated thing, thus highlighting the similarities between the two. For example, in the speech, the word "unbeatable" will function in the role of metaphor as it relates to things which the listeners are not able to overcome in their respective lives. It could be anything—smoking, fear of heights, eating addiction, postponing things, etc.

The technique for using this device is to *first* establish a metaphorical link between the word (that you want as your metaphor) and the core problem of your speech. *Then* ask a question to prompt the audience to think of an answer and therefore engage with what you are saying. Do not ask any question; ask a you-focused question. Hence, I used the word "unbeatable" as the metaphor. I selected this word because my audience can easily relate to this word in their lives, and asked a you-focused question based on that metaphor. The metaphorical transformation in our case study leads to the following question:

> Ladies and gentlemen, do you remember anything unbeatable in your life?

Here are a few ideas on selecting the best word (or phrase) as metaphor in your story. This word or phrase should be memorable. This word should also play an important role in your story. By doing this, you are relying on the memorability quotient of the word or phrase so the audience will draw meanings from the metaphor based on their own experiences.

To summarize, the first step is to identify a word or phrase as the metaphor. The next step is to use this metaphor as the main idea in a you-focused question.

… Transition… to childhood story

Transitions maintain a clear flow between the elements of your speech. Put simply, transitions are like escalators that smoothly move from one floor into another floor. You still realize that they are moving and there is a change in the course of things but not a sudden jolt. A cool way to transition into the second story would be to…

Transition Using Word Play and Metaphor

Did you observe that I used the word "remember" in the context setting? That's because I wanted to transition into my childhood story using that word "remember." An earlier version of the speech stated the context setting question as "What seems unbeatable in your life?" Well, this did the job of prompting the audience to think about the core problem, but the issue was that I was not able to do a smooth transition. I was searching for an answer to this transition. Then, I was watching a speech by Darren LaCroix that won him the World Championship of Public Speaking in 2001, where he set the context by asking, "Do you remember when you were down too long?" In that speech, "down" was the metaphor for failure and he was asking the audience whether they had been stuck in failure for a long time. Voilà! I found my transition word. So I modified the context setting statement to ask, "Do you remember anything *unbeatable* in your life?" Now, I transitioned using just two words: "I remember." Transitioning with as few words as possible is good. Then I made the transition even smoother by associating the metaphor "unbeatable" when introducing an important character (the antagonist) in my childhood story. The following sentences work as a transition to childhood story to introduce the antagonist and explain the metaphor "unbeatable" within the context of the story.

> I remember during my ninth grade, my classmate Vivek was unbeatable. I could never beat his rank in exams.

How Characters Create Connections

Now, that we transitioned into childhood story by introducing an important character (the antagonist), we need to describe the character in detail to the audience. Why? *This is where the connection happens.* The more they know about the character the easier they can connect. Audiences don't want to know only what happened, they want to experience the characters or places as your story comes to life in their mind. That's what turns on the light bulb in your audience member's mind. One super easy way to do this is to paint your character descriptions with vivid words that stimulate each of the five senses. You need to use words that make your audience feel as if they can actually see, hear, touch, taste, and smell what you saw, heard, touched (got touched upon), tasted, or smelled in your story. If your speech slot gets more time than my case study speech in this example, I would suggest that you utilize more words to deepen character descriptions. You can also bring more depth by being more specific in describing the appearance, voice, or behavior of the character. For example:

> Mike had blue eyes, brown hair, and wore rimless glasses. Him standing by my side, putting his hand on my shoulder, and saying "you are the best" gave me more energy than anything else…

In the above example, I've touched on the visual (blue eyes, brown hair, and rimless glasses), hearing ("you are the best"), and touch (putting his hand on my shoulder). After listening to such an introduction, your audience members feel that they know Mike personally. Can you see how powerful this could be?

You can use this technique not only for character description, but also to describe the scene or the setting. I have a word of caveat. Do not over use this device. In fact, while you are using any device or technique, your audience will suspect being manipulated by techniques employed solely to impress them. Instead, always focus on the real intent and value you want to provide your audience.

Creating Humor During Character Descriptions

After context setting and introducing the antagonist in the childhood story, I wanted to describe the character and I used this opportunity to create humor. Let me share what I did. I created a list with characteristics that are expected. These are the characteristics that people expect to hear. Then I created another list with characteristics that are not expected. These are the characteristics that people don't expect to hear. Then I used the Rule of Three, which we learned earlier to structure the humor creation process. I picked two characteristics from the first list: "big face" (expected) and "thick voice" (expected). I picked one from the second list: "a lot of cholesterol" (unexpected). "A lot of cholesterol" is used in a different connotation. My intent was to convey that he was a guy with too much false pride and not so easygoing. It worked! Here are the exact lines:

Vivek had a big face, a thick voice, and a lot of cholesterol.

Just try creating humor during character descriptions and see the results. It is a little bit of work. But it will be worth the effort when audiences are laughing and enjoying your speech.

CHAPTER 7

MY HUMOR THESIS AND SEVEN HUMOR DEVICES

In which you'll learn my thesis to maximize your success in creating laughs and seven key humor devices

Showing Conflict

That day—we got our results for our midterm exams. Vivek got fifth rank and I got fifteenth. Not surprising but depressing. Why? My classmates will think I am dumb, which I am, not. We guys started discussing our ranks and Vivek said, "I wonder how these guys end up in top three ranks." I said, "Vivek, even you can be in top three if you study harder." And he goes, "You can't even beat my rank. Just shut your mouth and leave." But in front of everyone, I got humiliated. I was furious.

Even though the above part of my speech shows the conflict in the childhood story, let us dissect how humor was infused into it. To do this, first, I want to talk about a practice/theory/ technique (whatever you may call it) that personally helped me create my number one strategy in maximizing the laugh lines. This is **combination of devices**. Even though it is hard to explain, I want to share this because I have tested this numerous times and I know this works. *The potential of any single device to create humor is less. However, the potential to maximize the success of creating and increasing the length of laughs is more when you combine the devices. The success of your laugh lines is directly proportional to the combination of devices you employ.* There are a number of advantages to be gained from combining the humor devices. The problem with using only one humor device is that an audience might be able to identify it and not react instantly. On the other hand, when you combine many devices, they are not easily distinguishable and your audiences cannot judge the individual laugh mechanics at work. The only choice is to enjoy your content. The moment you start combining devices, your success in creating humor increases exponentially; not only is the probability of your success insured, but also the intensity of your laughs.

The following part has seven powerful devices that can be used either individually or in combination with each other. As I said earlier, combination of humor devices is the key. Let us use the following part of the story to understand how perspective, empathy, self-deprecation, and contrast are combined to create laugh lines.

> That day—we got our results for our midterm exams. Vivek got fifth rank and I got fifteenth. Not surprising but depressing. Why? My classmates will think I am dumb—which I am, not.

Perspective

A story is not just a flat retelling of what happened. The audience wants to know it from your perspective. Let me explain the concept of perspective using the conflict part of the child-hood story. It was a simple story about my ninth grade incident. *We got our exam results. I got fifteenth rank. My classmate Vivek got fifth rank. Classmates started discussing ranks. I was feeling ashamed of my rank. I didn't want to be judged.* This is what happened. However, if you just say what happened, then your speech will become boring. This is very important because stories need to have different perspectives to make them interesting and entertaining. When you start saying things from different perspectives, you'll leverage this phenomenon to create humor.

How to create perspective:

Focus on a specific point in the story from different angles and provide an opinion through the eyes of a character present in the scene from a first person, second person or third person perspective. A specific point in time could be an eventful part of the story. This focal point is the "important thing" that happened in the story. Examples: your friend lost his job, you saw an accident in front of your eyes, you fell down trying to impress a good-looking girl, etc.

Now, if you are part of the scene in the story, say what you were thinking. Tell us what the other characters were thinking. Tell us what you were thinking about the other characters. Another idea is to make the perspectives match those of your audience members if they would have been in the same scene, in place of the main character. This is important because audiences always try to identify with the main character of a story. That's why the protagonist gets all the attention in any movie. When you start doing this perspective exercise, you'll get tons of ideas to help you create the twist required to create laughs. Let us see how this concept was used in my speech. Here's the "what happened" part of the story:

That day—we got our results for our midterm exams. Vivek got fifth rank and I got fifteenth.

This seems straightforward and clear. To illustrate from my perspective during that experience, I saw my character from the third person point of view. In this case, the character was feeling sad because his classmates would underestimate him because he scored a poor rank. The *character* didn't want to be judged this way, as is the case with the majority of people. No one really wants to be judged. Always keep anticipating how an audience will be reacting when forming perspectives. Then, communicate that perspective in a humorous way. Hence, I shared my perspective as the speaker, and then shared the perspective of me as the character. These are the exact lines I used:

> Not surprising but depressing. Why? My classmates will think I am dumb which I am, not.

Observe that I moved into the present tense to share my perspective. This helped me connect better. Do this, and you will have a real conversation with your audience. "Depressing" is a strong word that I used to set my context in an exaggerated way. Now, for the punch line:

> My classmates will think I am dumb which I am, not.

I love the above sentence because it came after a lot of rewriting. I used the devices of empathy, self-deprecation, and contrast, as well as modified Rule of Three to create this line. The audience enjoyed it so much that they applauded and I was thrilled. This is the sophistication of the humor derived from combining different devices.

Empathy

A good rule of thumb for crafting a story is to show the weakness of the protagonist. This is to make it easier for the audience to empathize with the character. When I wrote, "My classmates will think I am dumb," it was on the borderline of empathy and self-deprecation, not strong enough for an audience to laugh. However, there was opportunity to add a punch line. The secret is to add a relevant and unexpected punch line when the audience thinks the line is finished.

Self-Deprecating Humor

Self-deprecating humor entertains the audience by making you the target of the joke. Mind you, do not think you are losing self-respect by employing this device. In fact, your audience will respect you even more because you have the confidence and courage to talk about your vulnerability. Audiences love self-deprecating humor. Do some soul searching to find ideas where you can make fun of yourself. You'll be surprised to see how many ideas you'll get. In my case, I first added "which I am." Now, the laugh line became "My classmates will think I am dumb, which I am." This point of self-deprecation triggered the laugh.

I used yet another humor device to add another follow-up punch. Remember the secret: Add a relevant and unexpected punch when the audience is thinking that the line is over. Two things to keep in mind when adding follow-up punch lines are: One, the audience should laugh at your current punch line. Two, the second punch line needs to come pretty quickly. Hence, I added another punch using the next device: contrast.

Contrast

Contrast is a self-contradicting tool where your initial words convey one idea but the later words convey the opposite of what you meant initially. The beauty of this device is that it is naturally aligned to create humor because the contradiction becomes the twist, which is what we need to create punches. To create humor, you contrast with ideas in your punch lines to what was said in the premise. The easiest way to implement contrast is to use words such as "No," "Not," "Really?" "I was kidding" and "That was a joke." Moreover, the short and crisp words to implement contrast are the best ways to create punch lines. Coming back to our example: After combining contrast, the laugh line became:

> My classmates will think I am dumb which I am, *not.*

That additional word "not" got applause! This worked because I applied a modified version of Rule of Three, more like Rule of Four while delivering this piece. Let me explain.

Modified Rule of Three (Rule of Four)

Rule of Three is so powerful that even if you modify it, you get super results. Here's what I did. I divided the sentence into four parts:

First: My classmates will think

Second: I am dumb

Third (the unexpected twist): which I am

Fourth (the unexpected second twist): not

After hearing the fourth part, the audience got so delighted that they started applauding. Yay! *Getting applause in the middle of a speech is a moment you should strive to achieve.* When it happens, it is totally exciting!

Dialogue

Dialogue, like Rule of Three, is a communication device that can be used for multiple purposes:

- Dialogue comes in handy for shortening the length of a story without impacting its meaning.

- Dialogue can be used to convey the core message of your speech.

- Dialogue can be used as a *punch line* for your laugh lines.

Another secret to quickly create humor is through dialogue. You can set the right context to give the character the power to convey emotions and intentions through *dialogue*. Done well, this is the *point in time* where the *connection* with the audience will become strong.

Even off stage, you crack up because someone says something surprising. People are programmed to laugh this way. However, to be funny on stage, the premise has to be set clearly before you say the dialogue in your story.

For example, in the swimming story, when my dad was coaching me to swim, my thoughts were "should I really learn to swim from him?" However, to maintain the flow of the speech, I got creative and said it as a dialogue.

> He goes, "Do you want to learn swimming or not?" I said, "That's what I'm thinking."

The dialogue "That's what I'm thinking" is the punch line.

Here's another example to create humor by using dialogue:

> We guys started discussing our ranks and Vivek said, "I wonder how these guys end up in top three ranks." I said, "Vivek, even you can be in top three if you study harder." And he goes, "You can't even beat my rank. Just shut your mouth and leave."

See if you can observe how the conflicting situation was crafted to be insulting to the protagonist and still get away with the laugh. This explains the benign violation theory, which was introduced in Chapter 1. That theory is really helpful when designing dialogue for laugh lines. It will be funny only if any insult or harm to the character is benign, not malign. Dr. Peter McGraw and Joel Warner explain this concept in detail in the book *The Humor Code*. When I lack the time to test a laugh line, I use this same principle to gauge whether the laugh line might work or not. However, the best way to find if a laugh line works or not is to TEST it. Just deliver the laugh line to a group of people at a dinner or over coffee and see how they respond. If you get positive response, note it down. This will really help you create some smart and crisp dialogues for your speech.

Monologue

Monologues in this context are the "actual" thoughts that come to your mind during an experience. These thoughts can be used to create punch lines.

Monologue is a dialogue which you speak to yourself. How do you express this in a speech? One way is to write the monologue in the same way you would write a line of a dialogue and add "was like." So when you say "was like," it conveys intent, yet it does not mean you actually spoke those words. This works very well for first person. For example, "I was like, 'Really?'"

However, when you are creating monologues from second person perspective, then you can use "as if to say." For example, "He looked at me as if to say, 'You are stupid.'"

I hope you have come to understand how these techniques can help you create great punch lines. Now, let us continue with story-speech framework.

CHAPTER 8

CREATING HUMOR WITH OBSTACLES AND FIVE MUST-KNOW RHETORICAL DEVICES

In which you'll learn how to design obstacles in a humorous way and learn five must-know rhetorical devices to create humor and impact in storytelling

Creating Humor with Obstacles

All good movies or plays or TV programs make use of difficult situations. In fact, the obstacles are purposeful because these obstacles increase tension and interest in the story. It keeps the audience engaged at the edge of their seats. This part can be used to create humor. In order to do that, you need to create the premise by showing an anticipation of success in overcoming obstacles but then design a punch line when the protagonist fails to overcome obstacles.

Obstacles can be serious, which will make your audience cry. Or they can be made humorous to elicit laughter. The choice is yours. If you choose obstacles that will make your audience cry, please change your mind. Just kidding. Since the aim of this book is to show you how to create humor, let us stick to the same!

Let's see how I changed the obstacles in my story into laugh lines. A good story is crafted in a way so that the main character, the protagonist, tries various ways to solve the problem (or conflict) but fails and eventually succeeds with the help of a supporting character. This supporting character could be a friend, stranger, colleague, or family member or even a pet or an inanimate object such as a book.

This part of the story is the perfect time to create some humor. The audience is ripe to laugh because every attempt or step by the protagonist to solve the problem creates the expectation of *the problem being solved*. However, when you break that expectation by telling how things did not work, you'll create laughs. Setting the expectation and breaking that will result in laugh lines. You can go further and not only exaggerate how things did not work but also show how things got screwed up in a bad way.

People will connect with you when you share experiences and tell stories where you are looking for solutions but keep hitting obstacles. Why? Because this mirrors what happens in real life where nobody gets a fast solution. Let's see how to design obstacles. Picture a member of the audience in that situation to see if it rings true if they were in the same position. Then come up with obstacles. Let me show you how this is incorporated in the case study speech. I'll use the term *solution path* because the protagonist is on a journey to find a solution to achieve the goal.

<Solution path – asking friend for help> I went to my best bud-dy Rakesh and said, "I want to beat his rank. What do I do?"

<Obstacle – friend is acting as a pessimist > He said, "Forget it."

<Solution path – friend giving an idea> I said, "No." He said, "Okay. I have an idea. Why don't you study every day? You will become better. You can even beat his rank." I said, "Shall we start today?"

<Obstacle — friend only advised but did not give real support> He said, "No. No. You study, I have to play."

<Solution path – showing that I am determined to study. I selected my mom, sister, and friends because they are all relatable> That evening my friends called me to play cricket, I said "No." My sister called me to watch TV, I said "No." My mom called me to eat Maggi,

<Obstacle – temptation to have favorite food> I said, "Yes."

<Solution path – showing as if I studied for a long time> After eating, I picked up my book to study. I studied and studied and studied

<Obstacle – habit of feeling sleepy after I picked up the book to study> till I fell asleep after five minutes

Every line referenced as obstacle got a laugh. Solution path and obstacles is the part of the story where there is potential to uncover humor. However, you still need to use relevant humor devices to create laugh lines. Let's take the following sample as example:

My friends called me to play cricket, I said, "No."

My sister called me to watch TV, I said, "No."

My mom called me to eat Maggi, I said, "Yes."

As you know, I am a big proponent of combination of devices. I used contrast, dialogue, and rhetorical devices such as Rule of Three, alliteration, anaphora, and parallelism to make this work.

"No" is used to bring in contrast. However, the double-contrast "Yes" is creating the trigger for humor. Observe that *contrast* is embedded in the form of *dialogue*. Now, let us talk about use of rhetorical devices. Use of Rule of Three is pretty evident. The first two sentences pertain to "expected," "expected" but the third sentence pertains to "unexpected." The unexpected is created by the combination of double contrast and dialogue. Alliteration, anaphora, parallelism along with simile and epistrophe are rhetorical devices that I believe every speaker must know. Let us understand them while I still use the same example for reference.

Alliteration

Alliteration uses words starting with similar sounding syllables to have a pleasing effect on the listener. The words can be in close proximity or adjacent to each other in the sentence. This device is used so the audience is able to understand the words and their meanings clearly. It creates awe because the words are pleasing to hear.

To create humor, alliterations create a pattern and rhythm in the minds of the audience, thereby helping you engage and guide them in one direction. By now, you know that for laugh lines to work, there needs to be a change in direction. The beauty of alliteration is that it uses rhythm to keep the audience going in one direction, so they are off guard when the punch is delivered. Using alliteration is like using an additional processor that will increase the performance of your humor. This will enhance and increase the effect of humor because the audience remembers your words quickly. Check out the words in italics that form alliteration in our example:

My mom called *me* to eat *Maggi*

Another example from the swimming story to show the use of alliteration:

But my habits gave me that *pu*sh to *plu*nge into the *poo*l. I gasped for breath, fluttered my hands and legs as fast as possible, and I *s*tarted to *s*ink.

The premise leads my audience to the point where they expected the protagonist (me) to begin to swim. But I say the opposite "started to sink." In reality, I was not swimming either, hence the punch worked pretty well. Let's see how alliteration was used in the above sample. There were two usages. The first one "*pu*sh to *plu*nge into the *poo*l" created the rhythm and the second usage "*s*tarted to *s*ink" while maintaining the rhythm also created the surprise. The basic rule is not to lose track of the fact that all humor needs the element of surprise to work. Heightening the obstacles is a place in the story where you can introduce that surprise by using various humor devices.

Anaphora and Epistrophe

Anaphora means repeating the same words or word at the beginning of successive phrases or sentences.

Epistrophe is the opposite of anaphora. It uses the same word or phrase at the end of successive sentences.

From humor creation perspective, both these devices help us to shorten the premise. This is a very powerful editing tool as it can make a long story short.

In the sample, anaphora is "My... called me to" and epistrophe is "I said, 'No.'"

> My friends called me to play cricket, I said, "No."
>
> My sister called me to watch TV, I said, "No."
>
> My mom called me to eat Maggi, I said, "Yes."

Notice the pattern in which these sentences are constructed. This brings us to:

Parallelism

These are successive phrases written with similar grammatical structure to form a pattern and help the audience easily remember your ideas. Observe the sentences in the earlier example. One critical reason for using parallelism in humor creation process is to create rhythm, which creates a pattern in your premise, so that when you break that pattern by delivering the laugh line, the effect is pretty cool.

Simile

Simile is a device that compares one idea with another by using the words "like" or "as." The beauty of simile is that it allows us to simplify the explanation of a complex idea and adds variety, spice, and clarity to your speech.

Like other devices, simile also has multiple purposes, including creating humor. Simile works to create humor when the new idea being compared is way out of context yet draws some parallel. For example, in one of my speeches, I talked about my dad's rules at home which I compared with corporate policy. Here's what I said:

> My dad's policy is like a corporate policy. Both know what they want and then change the policy accordingly.

Now, that I have shed light on key rhetorical devices, please go back and review my usage in the other parts of the case study speech. Try to implement the same devices in your speeches; you'll thank me later.

CHAPTER 9

PERIPHERY AND SYNERGY OF MESSAGE

In which you'll learn how to: showcase change; wrap, uncover, and apply message; and use exaggeration as a humor device.

Showcase the Change

Your story will not create impact if you do not show the change in situation of the protagonist because audience members imagine themselves as the protagonist in your story. When you verbalize the change in situation of the protagonist, your audience will feel hopeful, delighted, and empowered by your story. This is the secret of the all-time hits. I'm switching to a movie example to prove this point. One of the movies which I cannot stop loving is *The Shawshank Redemption*. One of the core reasons it's so popular (it's ranked #1 in IMDB all-time hits list) is because of the change in situation of the protagonist. On a side note, the movie is worth watching! The more believably you showcase the change, the stronger the impact. I am saying this because after hearing the following lines, the audience was overjoyed and started applauding. Here's the part that showcases the change in childhood story:

I woke up and cried, again and again. I studied so that I could stop crying. And I studied every single day. After few months, exams came. Then the results came and guess what? Vivek got the sixth rank and I got the second rank in my class. My teacher was shocked. Vivek was shocked. I was shocked. It was like magic.

Wrap the Message

When you craft the "change" part of your story, spend some time and focus on the "how" part of it. In simple terms, this is the *plan* of the protagonist to overcome the obstacles and achieve the goal. Earlier, we learned how to heighten obstacles and show how things did not work. Now, you need to show how things worked. First of all, make sure you *wrap the message* when you are crafting the plan. Why? In order to create the curiosity in the audience to wonder "why" it happened. The next important point is that the *plan* should be believable. The following lines are the result of incorporating the above points.

I woke up and cried, again and again. I studied so that I could stop crying. And I studied every single day.

Later, we will learn at what point in the speech we can uncover "why" things worked and also learn how to uncover the message in your speech.

Avoid Bragging After Reaching the Goal

There are a couple of good reasons that I did not use a direct sentence such as "I beat Vivek's rank" and the first reason is to avoid bragging. The second reason is to communicate the idea that the protagonist excelled more than the expected goal.

The aim is to *show the change* in the protagonist's situation and the best way to do this is to have the character feel differently because of the change. You can craft the speech in such a way that either the protagonist or the supporting characters in your story *feel* differently. Hence, I used the words "It was like magic."

Exaggeration for Creating Humor

Since our aim is to look for the opportunity to create humor, let's see how it was done here by using *perspective* (introduced earlier) and *exaggeration* (which I am introducing now). When you show perspectives of different characters, humor is created. I used the following characters: my classmates, Vivek, and my teacher. Though my teacher was not introduced earlier, my audience was perceptive enough to assume there was a teacher present when we were talking about exams and results. *Exaggeration* does nothing but blow things out of proportion and is a great tool to use for punch lines. That's why I chose the word "shocked" even though "surprise" was an apt word for the following lines:

> My teacher was shocked. Vivek was shocked. I was shocked. It was like magic.

I'm again circling back to my thesis on combining the devices. You might be thinking that only the two tools of humor, perspective and exaggeration, are in play, but I had used two other rhetorical devices. One is the Rule of Three and the other is epistrophe, where the same word or phrase is used at the end of successive sentences. Check out the use of "was shocked." This device was very effective in creating short sentences to showcase different perspectives in an expanding timeline. In real time, the audiences were delighted after hearing the punch line "I was shocked." They cheered, laughed, and applauded. This is the type of stuff that elicits an emotional response.

Rule of Four

Rule of Four is an extension of Rule of Three but it has the power to create excitement about your message or any important point in your speech. Though Rule of Three was used in the recent example, it was use of Rule of Four that created excitement about the message. I said "It was like magic" as part four. That line described the feeling of the protagonist. The deeper idea was to connect that feeling of the protagonist to the word "magic," which was also the title of the speech. So that later, I can connect the *core message* to the *title* of the speech.

... Transition back to swimming story

I had to transition to the current storyline. The following was the sequence of actions that helped the transition.

- By verbally saying "Fast-forward fourteen years"

- By non-verbally walking forward a few steps

- By using the tap and transport technique. I first heard this technique from 1999 World Champion of Public Speaking Craig Valentine. This technique helps you to support and smoothen the transition and continue with your story. To implement this, you need to put the audience in the scene of your story. And then, describe the scene. Please observe the transition and the use of the tap and transport technique in the following excerpt:

Fast-forward fourteen years; if you were sitting with me in that coffee shop, you would have seen my best buddy Rakesh and me; sipping freshly brewed cappuccino and recalling that school incident.

Now, that the scene and context is set, you are free to recount the dialogues among the characters.

Uncovering the Core Message

In a speech, the key point and the core message can be one and the same. In my speech, that's what I did. There could also be up to three or four key points adding up to your core message. Either way works fine. In our case, the core message was "Habits Create Magic." Even though it sounds pretty simple, I burned a lot of calories trying to crystallize my message. Let's see how I conveyed the message.

Using Dialogue to Convey Message

Dialogue is a super cool way to convey your message. There are a couple of reasons for this. One is that you won't seem like you are preaching. The other is that you don't want it to seem as if you have all the answers. Even if you do have all the answers, you need not show the audience. This way, the audience will like you more because you don't seem like a know-it-all and you'll form a better connection with them. In the case study, let us look at where I used dialogue to bring out my message.

Rakesh said, "Do you know the exact reason for your magic at school?" I said, "Hard work." He goes, "No, it's because of your habit of studying every single day. Habits create magic."

Shortcut to Find Your Message

The following tip will help you create clarity for your core message. Practically speaking, finding a clear message evolves through the speech writing process. Let me explain. When I started, I had an idea that I want to talk about habits and hence I selected stories that could help me convey that message. If you are not sure what you want to talk about, there is a shortcut: *Write a story that you feel compelled to tell even though you are not able to synthesize the message out of it. Share it with people and ask, "What message did you get?"*

After getting feedback, process what the majority feels and see if it makes sense. In fact, this exercise will even help you get a catchphrase (I'll cover this soon). In my case, when I started my speech project, even though I knew that my message was about habits, I did not have "Habits create magic" as my catchphrase. Even though it seems to be a simple three-word phrase, it took me a lot of rewrites to zero in on that phrase.

Application of Core Message

Now, that you have clarified the message, it is imperative that you connect the benefits of that message to how it relates to the life of those in your audience. In fact, here's where doing audience research pays off. Beforehand, find what life solutions your audience members seek. When you connect the benefits of your message as the solution to problems in your audience members' life, then you'll make an impact. As a speaker, you'll hit a home run if you can empower your audience and make them confident that your message will solve their problems. When I delivered my speech to audiences of mostly corporate and business professionals, with a minor population of students, I used *metaphorical transformation* technique to achieve the same. I used the word "magic" as my metaphor for *benefits of implementing the message*. Every time I said "magic," my audience understood that I referred to *benefits of implementing habits*. Here's the excerpt:

> That's when it hit me—I was missing the magic of good habits in my life. I needed it badly to beat those things that seemed unbeatable. The question is—are you missing any magic in your life? It could be anything. Staying in shape, growing as a speaker, or being an ideal partner. For me, learning to swim was something I always wanted…

CHAPTER 10

CALLBACKS, REPETITION, AND POWER OF PAUSES

In which we'll learn how to use: callbacks for transition, repetition to increase intensity, and pauses to create segue laughs

Even though showing application of the message in the speech is not mandatory, doing it increases the chances that your audience will apply your message in their own lives. In my speech, after introducing and relating the message, I transitioned to my goal: learning to swim. In my story, I deliberately said things, which conveyed my persistence in trying to learn to swim. This helped in showing application of my message. However, I made sure that the essential elements of storytelling such as *obstacles, resolution,* and *change* were there. Observe the use of them in the following speech sample:

> Since childhood, swimming fascinated me but the water daunted me. Now my dad being a swimmer, I asked him to coach me. To make him say "Yes," I promised him that I would practice swimming for one hour every day. Sounds simple; yes. Was it easy? No. I struggled for seventeen consecutive days. And on the eighteenth day,

I stood on the edge of the long swimming pool. My hands were falling apart, my legs were falling apart, and the water was unbeatable. But my habits gave me that push to plunge into the pool. I gasped for breath, fluttered my hands and legs as fast as possible, and I started to sink. Even under water, I tried again and again and again. All of a sudden, I started floating. I beat the water, sprang to the surface and started beating on and on and on till I reached the far end of the long swimming pool. It was like magic.

Use Callback for Transition

Callbacks are words, phrases, or sentences that are repeated from the earlier part of a speech. These are generally used to create humor. However, I found this to be a useful tool to transition back to the earlier part of my story. The following callback transitioned me to the exact point in time when my swimming story began.

I stood on the edge of the long swimming pool. My hands were falling apart, my legs were falling apart, and the water was unbeatable.

The following is another callback present in the swimming story that helped the audience relate to the very same feeling created at the end of my childhood story.

It was like magic.

Here we saw callback as a transition device. In the 'Editing Strategies' chapter, we'll learn how to use callback as a humor device.

Use Repetition to Increase Intensity

Another thing I found to be really effective is to repeat words to increase the intensity of a situation. I want to point out that repeating words is not increasing your word count, repeating words is actually an economical way to use words to create an impact. However, you do need to spice up your delivery. Here's how I used repetition in a couple of instances in my case study speech:

I tried *again and again and again…*

… and started beating *on and on and on*

The Speech Summary

To summarize a persuasive speech is to combine the problem statement with the solution. The technique I used was to state specific solutions to the problems stated earlier in my speech. I got this idea while watching the winning speech of the 2013 World Champion of Public Speaking, Presiyan Vasilev, in Cincinnati, USA. I improvised my summary by adding epistrophe (repeating the same word or phrase at the end of successive clauses). See my use of the phrase "can create the magic" below:

What seems unbeatable in your life?

Maybe staying in shape seems unbeatable—a habit of working out 30 minutes every day can create the magic.

Maybe growing as a speaker seems unbeatable—a habit of competing in every speech contest can create the magic.

Maybe being an ideal husband seems unbeatable—a habit of saying "I love you" 50 times every day cannot create the magic. Listening to her 50 times can create the magic.

Power of Pauses to Create Segue Laughs

A habit of saying "I love you" 50 times every day *cannot create the magic*. Listening to her 50 times *can create the magic*.

The above sample is the *third part* of Rule of Three used during summary. With only these two sentences, I got three laughs and two rounds of applause. Even though combination of contrast and Rule of Three devices laid the foundation, the *pause* played a vital part in getting segue laughs (where I get laughs after every word or so). The main reason: We are giving time for the audience to imagine themselves being in that situation. It's just amazing how pauses help you do that. Here's how it worked out:

A habit of saying "I love you" <pause> 50 times <pause> every day <pause> *cannot create the magic <pause>*. Listening to her 50 times <short pause to build tension> *can create the magic <pause>*.

Every pause after "I love you," "50 times," and "every day" got laughs. When I said the contrasting statement "cannot create the magic," audiences started applauding. When I paused after "listening to her 50 times <short pause> can create the magic," audiences again started cheering and applauding.

Speech Conclusion

Conclusion is the final 30 or 60 seconds of a speech. It's your chance to make the audience remember your speech. Though you might give a stellar speech, you might miss your chance to hit a home run if you do not end strong. There are many ways to conclude a speech. One age-old technique is the solution close. This helps the audience relate the problem to their own life and reminds them of the solution one final time.

In the case study, this was achieved by using metaphor and catchphrase. Since swimming pool was a main element in my story, the swimming pool was used as a metaphor for life. I chose the words "fall apart," "struggle," and "sink" from the swimming story as metaphors for problems in life. Takeaway: Always choose words from the story that can relate directly to audience members' lives. The solution was summed up with the catchphrase "Habits create magic." I'll talk about catch-phrase and catchword soon, as they need to be discussed from a complete speech perspective. For now, think of them as a word or combination of words that you want the audience to take away from your speech and remember even a few years down the line. To make your conclusion even more effective, you can actually make the audience repeat the catchphrase or the catchword. I said the conclusion in a sincere and passionate manner and paused before saying the final catchword "magic." In fact, I let my audience say "magic." It is a great feeling when your audience says the catchword. You have a proof that they got the message. Here's my conclusion:

Friends, in the swimming pool of your life, you might fall apart; you might struggle; you might even sink, in the water that seems unbeatable. But you can beat the unbeatable using habits because "habits create magic."

CHAPTER 11

ELEVEN EDITING STRATEGIES

In which you'll learn eleven editing strategies for creating a tight script

"Rama, a tight script is one where you use around 3,000 to 4,000 words to come up with a 1,200-word script," said my mentor Jerry Aiyathurai. It was an aha moment for me. The more I worked to create tight scripts, the better I understood the significance of his wise words. If you have read Lincoln's Gettysburg Address of only 272 words, you'll see what began as a longer speech was tightened to its core essence. The one core strategy that created this masterpiece is the magic of editing. That's why editing plays a major role in creating any successful movie, book, poem, story, article, or speech. This chapter covers the granular editing strategies I use to create a tight script. I am sure this will help you as well.

Shorter Premise, Greater Impact

The length of the laughter after punch line is inversely proportional to the length of the setup in premise. This means that the information in your setup to the audience should be *just* enough for them to appreciate your punch line. Please chew on and take the time to digest this statement. What it means is that when you sit down to edit, this should be your guiding principle. Your setups need to be clear and brief. Trim down all unnecessary parts in the premise that do not add any value to the story.

Let me give one more perspective. *Your premise need not be a set of words.* It could be non-verbal, or a combination of non-verbal and verbal communication. Instead of words, consider using facial expressions and body movements to set up your premise. I'll give an example. In one of my stories I had an idea to create humor during the orientation of the scene. As you'll remember, orientation is the why, what, when of the scene. My idea was to orient the audience to a scene where my dad and I were sitting at home. My plan for humor was as follows:

Plan for premise: Audience should think that my dad and I were boozing.

Plan for punch line: Contrast that thought by letting them know that we were just having tea.

To set that premise, I said: "On a Friday evening, my dad and I—we were having a good time." When I said "having a good time," I did body movements like a drunkard. Then, after the pause, I delivered the punch line, "We were having tea." This laugh line works almost 99 percent of the time.

Use Crisp Dialogue

As a speechwriter you need to craft succinct and clear dialogues. This means that to be a good speaker, you need to be a good writer. As we learned earlier, using dialogues reduces the number of words in the story and gives an opportunity to call out the message in the speech. But dialogue is also useful in creating humor because it serves as punch lines, and editing helps in creating effective punch lines. While editing, cut back on dialogues that go back and forth too many times. If you want to keep an exchange of dialogue more than twice, you need to make sure that the audience is clearly following through during your delivery. And also, make sure that only necessary words that *convey ideas* are present in your dialogues. For my case study, I had edited not to have dialogue exchanged more than twice or dialogues that are too long or wordy.

Not New, Renew Your Punches

By now, you should have a good idea about storytelling and humor. Which is better? Creating premise/punch followed by a new premise/punch or creating premise/punch followed up by another punch line? The answer is to create a follow-up punch line instead of starting a new premise/punch. This can be done only during editing. It is then that you can uncover the extra punches or combine ideas to form follow up punch lines. When you deliver any laugh line, sit and think about new ideas that connect to the same. Let's take an earlier example that illustrates the application of this principle.

> Ramakrishna Reddy is not my complete name. Actually my name in passport says, "Ramakrishna Reddy Veerappa Narayana Reddy." Do you know what is hard about having a long name? People make fun of you. Few months ago, I was at New York airport and the officer looked at my passport and goes, "Ramakrishna Reddy

Veerappa Narayana Reddy. Sir, it seems you have used all alphabets in English language."

In this case, we can add follow up punch lines and continue the story by using monologue or dialogue from another character to create humor.

I usually go with what happened in a real experience and choose a suitable device. In the real experience, I thought "Moron, that is not funny… and also I thought… It was all because of my dad." So, I polished these two thoughts into a proper monologue. I also used "mind" to differentiate between them. Here's the follow-up punch line:

> Hearing that, one part of my mind goes, "Moron, that's not funny" and the other part of my mind goes, "Daddy, why me?"

Observe, that the punch words "Daddy, why me?" are crisp and convey the intent of what I wanted to say. This way we leveraged an earlier punch line to create new punch lines in the story.

Punch Words Should Come Last

Check out these sample laugh lines in the case study speech.

> My dad is kind and patient with everyone *except me.*

> Fluttered my hands and legs as fast as possible and *started to sink.*

> Studied and studied and studied till I fell asleep after *five minutes.*

Do you think these lines were written the first time I drafted the speech? No! It takes a lot of rewrites and tweaks to frame proper punch lines. It is very important that the words that trigger the surprise should always be the *final words* in the sentence. This means, while editing, rewrite the sentences and put the punch word or phrase towards the end of the sentence.

Create Crisp Contrasts

We have covered contrasts. Here I'm reiterating the editing technique. After writing your speech, go over it and try to find contrasting scenarios and replace them with contrasting words such as "no," "not," "Really," "I was kidding," "True story," etc. These are clear contrasts. Contrast can be done in the context of the story as well. For example, check the following:

> I go home, I picked up the book to study. I studied and studied and studied till I fell asleep after five minutes.

"Studied and studied and studied till I feel asleep" is the premise that creates the thought that I studied for a long time but "after five minutes" is the punch line that contrasts the premise, creates humor, and gets the laugh.

Iteration Is the Key

Chuck out any laugh lines that do not get a response. However, keep those with even a feeble response and analyze them. Determine whether it is the premise or the punch that is weak. Then, strengthen where needed by adding or removing words. Sit with anyone and brainstorm different punches and watch for the best reaction in the other person. If they laugh or smile involuntarily, you have a winner. Most of my laugh lines eventually became better because I did this.

Simplicity Is the Best Policy

Were you the person who everyone looked up to for the use of high-end vocabulary? Well, it's good to be that person but it is not true that using flowery and complex words will portray you as a great speaker. Speaking is not prose. You get only one chance for your listener to understand you. If you lose them even once, you lose them completely for the rest of the speech. In order to create an effective listening experience, replace complex, ambiguous, and unusual words with short and simple words. These should be words that we use in day-to-day communication. And also, there could be words that just do not roll off your tongue. Do not force it. Just refer to www.thesaurus.com and replace that word.

Design Callbacks

The callback references an earlier idea or line in the speech and when it is used correctly gets you the big laughs. Let us have fun learning how to do this. We can create humor using a line or word that was referred to earlier in the speech. Usually, the line or word already got a laugh. However, even if that was not funny (not intended to be funny in the first place), if you use it later on (it should come as a surprise) as a callback, it can create a laugh.

Callbacks are often uncovered during the editing process. In one of my speeches, I told a story about working in a busy office when my girlfriend called me. She started a fight by saying that I don't call her enough (side note—why do they say this all the time?). My response was to yell at her, using the dialogue: "Don't you know how hard I am working? Don't you know how important my role is?" Her response: "Yes, I know how important your role is, idiot." When the audience heard "idiot," I got a laugh. At a later part in the speech, there was another situation where I could have picked a fight but instead I chose to say, "I am sorry. Please don't make this an issue." And she says, "I... I am making an issue. What do you think, Rama? You say sorry and I will forgive you?" I pause and say to the audience: "Now, I really felt like an idiot." This gets an even bigger laugh. The laugh was bigger because of the callback to the earlier reference of "idiot."

Here's another example from our case study. In the first paragraph, my dad said, "Jump." I did not get a laugh. However, when I repeated "Jump" again, I got a laugh. Usually, you do not use a callback so early. There were other things such as voice modulation, dialogue, and exaggeration that aided in getting that laugh, however, the callback of the word "Jump" was the main reason for the laugh.

Design the Catchphrase

A catchphrase is a very powerful device that the audience remembers long after the speech is over, sometimes for years to come. "I have a dream" by Martin Luther King Jr. is a catchphrase that still lingers in the minds of many people even though it was spoken decades ago. The phrase "Yes, we can" spoken by Barack Obama during his presidential campaign still lingers because it was a catchphrase. These two powerful examples show the impact and importance of using a catchphrase or catchword. Let's see how to design one. Choose simple words that encapsulate your core message or choose words that act as a metaphor to signify the message. In the case study, "Habits create magic" was the catchphrase and "magic" was the catchword. You can refer to the speech to understand the usage and impact.

Clarity of Timeline, Clear Flow

The timeline is the backbone of the story. If you do not get this right, you will end up confusing or boring your audience. When you are telling a story, you are either expanding or contracting a point in time.

By default, we naturally *expand the timeline* when telling a story because it is what we see and experience. However, to be a good storyteller, you need to learn to describe a situation of extended duration in few sentences. This means to contract what happened over a month or year into a few lines. Being able to do this will add pizzazz and shine to your speech. In my childhood story, there was a need to contract the timeline from *day of nightmare* to *day of change* in the protagonist's life. The following is an earlier version.

> I studied so that I could deviate from the nightmare. After a few weeks, I started getting excited about studying. It was a nice feeling. I soon looked forward to study every evening. Then, the exams were announced. I studied with full vigor and gave the exam. I was so nervous while giving exam that my hands were shaking. We went for holidays and when we returned to school, the first day

we were about to get the results. I was so nervous to get the marks. I collected the marks for every subject from my teacher. Then the results came and the results were surprising. I got second rank and the guy who humiliated me got a lower rank. I was really surprised because I only wanted to beat the rank of my classmate. However, I excelled and stood among top three.

Even though the above piece of story is good, the same meaning can be conveyed in fewer words. Moreover, it can be made humorous as well. The essence of the above is *I studied hard every day. In the next examination, I got a better rank than my classmate Vivek.* In this case, our task is to contract the time period from the day the protagonist started getting nightmares to the day the protagonist achieved his goal.

To do this, I recommend "short sentences" as your editing tool of choice. Every short sentence should represent a connecting idea. When these are used in sequence, the whole time period is covered. After much thought, the following key words represented the ideas that I needed to convey in contracting time: *studied every day, exams, results.* These ideas need to be present in the contracting timeline whereas *beating Vivek's rank* and *It felt like magic* needed to be present in the expanding timeline. See the sequence of the following short sentences.

> "I studied every single day. After few months, exams came. Then, the results came. And guess what?"

See, how quickly I glazed over the months? In fact, I became ready for the scene where I was able to talk about expanding timeline. If you were eagle-eyed, you spotted the use of the rhetorical device epistrophe. The word "came" used at the end of the successive sentences is an epistrophe that helps to focus only on the ideas *exams* and *results*. Guess why "guess what" is used. It is for transition so that we can talk about ideas in the expanding timeline. Just to be clear, expanding timeline is the experience in a particular scene or simultaneous experiences at the same second or minute. The "short sentences" for expanding timeline were:

> My teacher was shocked. Vivek was shocked. I was shocked. It was like magic.

Let Go, to Let the Speech Grow

Sometimes we start off with a brilliant line and as we continue editing the speech, it evolves into something more. Now, that initial brilliant line doesn't work. For example, in my earlier version of my case study speech, I had a line that read, "Habits could be the bridge between your desires and results." A lot of people loved it and so did I. However, as the speech evolved, I could not fit that sentence anywhere. So, I removed it. It was painful. But hey, that's okay. Sometimes, we just need to let go, to let the speech grow on its own. The fundamental idea is this: Even if you love a specific line, specific story, or a specific anecdote, if it does not add value to your key message, get rid of it.

CHAPTER 12

TWELVE EXECUTION STRATEGIES

In which I'll cover twelve strategies to connect with story and humor in a persuasive speech

Warm Up Your Audience

In stand-up shows, opening acts warm up the audience for the main artist. Our case is different. In most cases, there is no one to warm up your audience. Your only warm-up tool is humor. What I mean is, your opening laugh lines actually function to warm up the audience. When you set the proper mood, you will have the audience on your side. So, it is very crucial you get that first laugh as soon as you can.

Be Clear with Your Laugh Lines

Identify the premise and punch for every laugh line you want to create and run each through the insights of premise, pause 1, punch, and pause 2.

You need to clearly know where your laugh lines are. If *you* are not clear where to expect the audience to laugh, the audience will not be clear either.

Never Say It's Coming

A common problem for speakers trying to create humor is to say things like "I am going to tell a funny story" or "something funny happened." Please don't do that. The audience will unconsciously build resistance to laugh. If they predict it, then you might not get the laugh. I faced this issue because I smiled before delivering my punch lines. This facial expression was acting as a clue to the audience, which ruined my surprise punch lines. A good friend pointed this out and I had to practice hard to stop smiling. When I succeeded in controlling my smile, my response level increased.

Internalize the Content

The age-old problem in public speaking: How do you remember the content? Is it a good idea to memorize every word by heart and recall on stage? No! The secret to a flawless execution is to internalize an entire speech. That's when you'll rule the stage. To do this, keep practicing your speech over and over till you don't have to consciously think about saying it. When you do this properly, at some point in time, you will just open your mouth and the words will flow. The other term for internalizing is called muscle memory. It's hard to explain the power of muscle memory. It is just an amazing feeling when the words, body movement, and voice are in unison and you have complete control over the speech. In fact, because of the confidence that will result from muscle memory, your body movements and voice modulation will become smooth. Muscle memory has to be experienced in order to understand its depth and power.

Be Intelligible

When my mentor Jerry said, "Rama, you will be a stronger speaker if you are intelligible," I was thinking, "Is he saying that I have to be intelligent?" He is so smart that he instantly knew that I did not understand what he meant. He continued, "Rama, you'll be effective as a speaker when 99% of the audience understands 99% of your speech." That in a nutshell is intelligibility. Knowing and striving for it can prove to be a complete game changer for you as it did for me. Audiences can clearly understand what you are saying only when they can hear and understand the meaning of your words. It is then that you will get your desired response.

Keep Listener in Visual Mode

As a speaker, you must help the audience visualize your story. This is a main channel for your audience to stay connected during a speech. When punch lines are delivered in this visual state, they are really effective. It doesn't matter if the punch lines are slapstick or thought-provoking humor.

Modulate Your Voice

Voice modulation is an important element that cannot be overlooked when you are storytelling. In fact, this is a foolproof tool to help you convey a larger meaning of your statement. Use a higher pitch, a lower tone, or a little more exaggeration when delivering certain words or phrases to add a whole new flavor or attitude to a sentence. The following are some easy to remember secrets to use during storytelling.

Secret 1: When using a dialogue, you say things such as "I said" or "he said" and continue with dialogue. 1999 World Champion Craig Valentine gave a cool tip on this and I found it to be very effective. He advises to glaze over the "I said," "he said" and concentrate on voice modulation when saying the actual dialogue. I have personally used this tip and it works great! This subtle technique will make a huge difference between you and the other speakers.

Secret 2: Try to associate a specific and distinctive voice to each character. This is an effective way of clearly differentiating a character to an audience. This does not mean to mimic a character. For example, if you are a guy, you need not mimic a girl's voice. However, you should vary your voice to clearly differentiate a girl in the dialogue.

As a general rule of thumb, imagine being the character and let the character's emotion take its course by modifying your body language and mannerisms. This trick can be used for any character whether an old person, a small kid, or a strict dad. Just imagine the character in that situation and say the dialogue. The audience will easily connect.

Secret 3: Inflections during punches will accentuate laughs. The punch word must be inflected to give a vocal change of direction. This compounds the effect that your punch creates in the minds of the audience. This is the kind of stuff that turns a good laugh line into a great laugh line.

Internal Excitement

If there is one winning tip, it is to remain *excited* during the speech. Every time I follow this advice, it has worked wonders.

When I forget this simple strategy, I pay the price. But, I can confidently say that projecting excitement helps you rock the stage. Before the audience can enjoy the humor quotient, you have to enjoy it. When you do that, excitement builds naturally and you'll be eager to take the stage. Excitement is not about just showing it externally; it is about *feeling* it internally.

Be Cool with Hecklers

Once when I was auditioning for a corporate gig, there was a pair of hecklers sitting in the second row making loud comments and disturbing everyone including me. Unfortunately, I showed my anger on stage. I swore at them and left the stage. Who lost? Well, it's me. It is clearly not the best way to deal with the situation. Hecklers are the people in an audience who criticize, comment, and distract the speaker for no reason except to attract attention to them. Either they are mentally unstable, or they are testing your skills. Good news is that hecklers are few. The larger crowd always wants the speaker to do well. If hecklers appear in your audience, remain cool and don't give them any attention. Soon the rest of your audience will also grow tired of them and will support you.

Gaining Back Train of Thought

It happens to all of us; sometimes we lose our train of thought during a presentation. The reasons for this are many. Maybe we saw someone in the audience and got distracted, or maybe nerves got the upper hand. When this happens and it will, please do not blame yourself. Here's what happened to me. I was supposed to speak at 5:45 p.m. on a Saturday at a meeting that started at 5 p.m. I left home for the venue and picked up a few friends on the way. I reached the venue parking at 5:42 p.m. (thanks to the insane amount of traffic!) and entered the meeting hall at 5:45 p.m., exactly at my time slot. Even before I could adjust to being on stage, I began with my opening: "I've known Jim since 2009. At that time, he was a big man. Even now he is a big man, physically. To describe Jim in one line—Jim is like a 120-liter Coca Cola bottle opening happiness wherever he goes." After that, I was supposed to say, "Jim did not pay me to say this. He is a great trainer and an awesome coach. You can contact him if you want coaching for prepared speeches, impromptu speeches, or finding a girlfriend." However, I lost my train of thought and missed my actual line. But I managed to fill in with a stock line and said, "That's it. I am done." People laughed. It gave me time to get back on track so I could continue: "Good evening, ladies and gentlemen, today you are going to walk away with three lessons I learned from Jim."

Strategies for getting back on track:

- Have a couple of stock lines in muscle memory that you can use when you lose your train of thought.

- When you forget, do not try to go back, just forge ahead, your audience will never know. I missed a great one during my speech but if I had tried to recall it, it would have ruined the flow of my talk and called attention to the fact that I made a mistake.

- Internalize the *structure* of your speech. Do this and you'll always know at which point of the presentation you are. You won't lose track even if you forget a few words.

Turn Distractions into Humor

During a live speech, situations arise which were not planned. These can either fluster you or you can turn them to your advantage.

The best possible way to handle distractions is *not to get flustered*. Trust that your audience will empathize when there is a problem. Respect that and continue with your presentation. As you get comfortable on stage, you can channelize these distractions into humor. Let's learn how to convert the three most common distractions into humor.

Power Shuts Down:

If power shuts down or PowerPoint does not work, or the microphone goes dead, just be cool. Use this opportunity to say something light-hearted.

I saw this happen in our corporate town hall. The entire power supply went dead, except for the microphone. The speaker continued by saying, "The microphone works. So, I will continue and my head will probably reflect all the light you need." He was bald. The entire hall erupted with laughter.

If you are part way through the presentation and the power shuts down, try saying, "I think we need a break" or come up with something on your own.

In any situation where there is a disturbance that affects both you and your audience, by default the audience will look up to the speaker for a solution. I don't know why this happens but that's the fact. If it's a technical issue, keep entertaining them until the organizers fix the issue.

Cell Phone Ringing:

This is a very common scenario these days. Be prepared with one or two comeback lines so you're ready when it happens to you. If the cell phone ring did not disturb your presentation, then ignore it. If you feel it did, create some humor around it. For instance, Craig Valentine in one of his audio programs used the following line: "Please tell your friend that I will call him later."

The above line seems to be teasing the person but that's okay as long as you show the intention to have some fun. You can come up with your own lines and keep them ready.

Latecomer to Your Presentation:

People walking in late is more common than you think—so be prepared. When it happens, choose to ignore it and act as if nothing happened. This is a good idea if the person sneaked in without disturbing the flow of your presentation. If this person does hamper the flow of your presentation, then you can slightly tease that person and create some humor. Stand-up comedians use lines such as: "Welcome, we were just waiting for you" or "Do you need something… like a watch?" The reason you need to tease the person disturbing the flow of presentation is because that person just stole the attention from you. Hence, to regain it, you need to acknowledge the disturbance by teasing or cracking up a line or so and continuing with your presentation.

Review to Improve

After you complete writing, rehearse and record your speech using video. Then, review the video. You'll discover use of some mannerisms that may surprise you. Correct those mannerisms that do not communicate the intended ideas. Repeat and rinse the same process for the actual presentation as well. The following pointers will help you kick off the review process.

Audience response:

> Did they smile, or laugh or applaud to your laugh lines?
>
> Did they nod or acknowledge rhetorical questions?
>
> Did they reply to any reciprocal questions?
>
> Did they remain engrossed throughout the speech?

Mannerisms:

> Did you have repeated hand gestures?
>
> Did you have unwanted movements?
>
> Did you cover the audience with proper eye contact?

Voice Reception:

> Are you *mumbling* your words?
>
> Are you *dashing* words with each other?
>
> Are you speaking without any pause?

There will be many more key insights you might get when you review your video recording. Recording will go a long way to answer any of the above questions and will be your key to take your speech to the next level.

Bonus Chapter. Case Study Speech Video Link and free Audiobook

In which you'll see a video link of the case study speech and also the speech script with the laugh lines and applauses marked for reference.

Case Study Speech Video Link

www.publicspeakking.com/connect-case-study

I had removed a few laugh lines in this version to cater to the time limit for the contest. There are other versions where I got laughs for the ones indicated in the below script.

Download Audiobook:

Please visit www.publicspeakKing.com/connecttopic and download the *Public Speaking Topic Secrets* audiobook. This will enhance your game of public speaking.

CONCLUSION

I have learned that *being coachable* is a key trait that successful people show. You have shown that trait. Congratulations and thank you for completing the book. I am so happy that you took the effort to learn about humor and story to improve your game of public speaking.

As I was finishing this book, I read a beautiful book, *So Good They Can't Ignore You* by Cal Newport. Cal's point is that you need to get good before you can produce good work. I cannot agree more. Getting good at humor and stories may take some time but once you achieve this skill, you'll sizzle on stage. You probably will not be able to incorporate all the ideas at once. Focus on one thing at a time. You might get afraid that your ideas won't work. That's okay. Only when things don't work will you really understand how to make it work. Come back and read again. You'll appreciate things which missed your attention earlier. Imagine the audience cheering, laughing, or applauding. Trust in yourself and you'll do well.

The real thrill will come for me when you start seeing these results. I'd love to hear from you. Either share your thoughts directly with me at Rama@PublicSpeakKing.com or kindly leave a review at www.amazon.com so that it will help someone like you to know more about this book.

Keep Smiling, Keep Rocking, and Happy Public Speaking.
Wishing You Success,
Ramakrishna Reddy
www.ramakrishnareddy.com

Made in the USA
San Bernardino, CA
30 January 2019